THE GRIEF
WE'RE GIVEN

POEMS

WILLIAM BORTZ

2021

Published by Central Avenue Publishing, an imprint of Central Avenue Marketing Ltd.
www.centralavenuepublishing.com

THE GRIEF WE'RE GIVEN

Cloth: 978-1-77168-219-0
Epub: 978-1-77168-220-6
Mobi: 978-1-77168-221-3

Published in Canada
Printed in United States of America

1. POETRY / General   2. POETRY / Grief

10 9 8 7 6 5 4 3 2 1

for chelsie and casey

CONTENTS

God, I have touched the living face of a person
I love with the same hands I have touched the
dying face of someone I love and none of that
seems fair.

—Hanif Abdurraqib

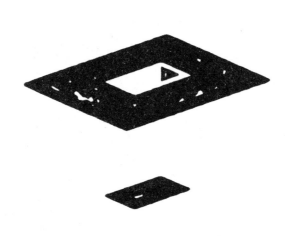

IN ALL MY MEMORIES FLOWERS ARE TAKING THE PLACE OF FACES

instead of telling you my name / I will unravel my hands from my pockets and show you what I have lost / those little eternities know me best / they dig their eager claws into my tender belly and call me to be hungry / I am not ready / I am a removal / I often do not believe morning when it tells me it will arrive with newness in its small mouth / like the steady light of home turning the front porch into a lighthouse / I am uncertain / so do not consider it a blade to your throat / when I tell you that I am unsure if our eternity will outlive the others / give pain a body / and it will press your arm between your shoulder blades / until you cannot hold who you love anymore / I've given pain a whole country / I have tilled its fields and fed the children / until they were plump and perspiring / I fashioned crude knives from steel / and taught them to dance with the killing thing resting patient in their teeth / something I meant to learn myself / I've waited and waited and waited so long and now all I know is surrendering / I am frail and bleached / now I eat only what pain gives me / and slowly / in cool, fragmented light / I am forgetting your face

grief —

an unfastening—an in-
a question, open and
standing beneath a
the inability to
the infallible wisdom
do you enter—
of a fading breath

evitable mechanic of humankind
spilling, begging to be answered—
waterfall in hope of getting just a mouthful
unremember etched into bone.
of suffering—leading to an open door
do you press your palm to the chest
and wait for stillness.

OCTOBER, AND EVERYTHING IS BREATHING

God—

are you only a noise

tall, dry reeds battering

the wooden fence keeping

the leaping prairie

within its own riot

can one breath from

the eternity of your tongue

calm a country

if so, could you

recite my name

BIRTHDAY

have you ever felt inspiration from something ceasing / once, I saw a bird collapse out of the blueness it was once kept in / it plummeted, in silence, and I thought how nice it would be to find rest on this afternoon / I am mostly enthralled in newness / when I am chained to something / unmoving / I baked my mother a cake on her 57th birthday / because I believed it would be her last / and that her own hand would bring the sort of bitterness to her mouth / that her heart could not survive / each birthday before / we were sure the call / the one that echoes / would ring out / ironically, as a morning bird / greeting a new day / and it would be new / in the way fresh absence swallows sunlight and time and half of every / breath we take / I never thought of her as a / bird / but as the sky that once held me / I am the bird / and no one has ever made me a nest / not even for one night / not even on my / birthday

WITHOUT

there is little to say aside

from out of all the heaviest

words to carry this one

is & is without skin

so it cannot be dragged

but carried in both arms

THERE'S GOT TO BE MORE TO A HUMAN BEING THAN THAT

but I cannot seem to find space for much more
than stiff wire and soft bone
all action and reaction
how could a soul ever
latch on to this shrapnel
maybe there is nothing but chemistry here
I take a breath—carbon
I hold my wife's hand, brittle as a bumblebee—carbon
she folds her body like paper
I inhale the smoke from her teeth
we unwrap her together and feed
our child—carbon
this small breathing thing
delicate as a sacrifice
a nickel-sized longing
is all this essential for life
each day I am decomposing so rapidly
I am made of expanding ghosts
we sit on our porch ruthlessly aging
watching our child watch what is watching her
a robin dragging its bad wing on the pavement
a dusk spilling open only to be closed
her eyes widen, the bird flaps its good wing
she coos—carbon

BLADE OF GRASS

hand in hand

hands by side

hand outstretched, finger extended, pointing to the yawning dusk-moon

lips pursed

lips closed

lips spilling with laughter

drinking honey from the river

drinking the river from palms

drinking starlight wrung from clothing

eyes soft

eyes scanning cylinders of clean light for dust

eyes scanning veins of leaves

eyes outlining the flower blossoming in the garden behind your ear

hair down, still wet

hair up, *a temple*

hair caught in the wind, painted gold and hot

hair strand [your], pinned between the skin of my back and my shirt,
    pulled out slow, feels like a ribbon of light casting a shadow on my
    neck

voice thick as honey

voice airy as lemon water

voice [your] speaking to the back of my throat

voice carrying my name over street-sounds

voice planting sunflowers in my palm

voice sultry in summer, dripping with wonder

bones [your] stretched over with lavender, pulled taut with
        morning dew

bones laying down pavement, ivory sidewalks to the end of the world

bones [our] making gunsmoke, asking the rain to paint us into
    the country

bones [your] bent over the young plant in the kitchen, watering,
    watering, water—

blushing moon watching through a coin of light

blushing flower in April, in the shade, in the point of your eye, on the
    corner of your mouth

blushing morning sun, open and spilling like a question

forearms folded into an origami swan gliding over still water, pandering
    to the infinity-feel of a July afternoon

forearms rubbed with the head of a dandelion, running like bruises to
    the pit of the elbow, color pulled from skin by latching together
    like a hinge

forearms adorned in keyholes of light seeping out from puncture
    wounds in the blanket of a night sky

sun-drenched, light-drunk, toothy smile, mouthful of wine,
    sleep until nine

sun-kissed ear resting in the shade of my shoulder, the aloe in quiet, the
    soothe of space

sun-tendered palms, warm as high-rising clouds kissing the chin of a

        dusk-moon, pressed to my cheeks, planting roses
        in the high bones, closest to dayrise, closest to moonbeams
        closest to your navel, close to sleep, close to tomorrow, close to
        more, red spilling over the stars peppering the landscape at two
        in the morning, close to [your] bones

the candle in the corner painting [us] into one cloud on the wall

the movement of intimacy being not where a blade of grass could be
    placed between our bodies but how far away [we] are from
    everything else

intimacy—

delicate and hungry, like a gun beneath a pillow.

OUTCOMES

I am scared of outcomes
terrified that they
happen whether I will them

to or not. frightened of
all the petals left to
wilt in warm palms.

love, of all things, is a
haunting. how do you
keep exuberant things

close to you without them
becoming a shadow—
even now, I am growing
dim.

death will forever
be the enemy
because it will take

and have the audacity
to force me to watch
when the only outcome I

desire is to be the petal
and not the palm.

TONIGHT NOTHING'S WORSE THAN THIS PAIN IN MY HEART

after "El Paso" by Marty Robbins

I move pretty quickly when I am giving distance / between myself and the man with the gun / he, who is giving more value to the ground he stands upon than I do / that man being anything that doesn't have a definable face / a people, a tremble, a machine / I can keep everything I know to be holy in my mouth / names, fingers, stray strands of chocolate hair / my life exists in their thin and frail shadow / and I open my eyes each morning / only to kneel in wake of their breath / if you sculpt a monument from sand / that too / I will revere and call to be moist and tame beneath my tongue / if you call me to be, I will flow outward and become a river / a terribly raging thing / almost always a pair of starving hands cannot finish what they wished to begin / almost always something is left half-alive and writhing / *almost always* / I once cowered within danger's shadow as it stood, rapping at my door / but now I have become that which knocks / I called distance to be a sea / and drank an entire ocean / I have become that faceless thing guarding hallowed ground / I imagine a bullet is fired each time I take a breath / and it is hard to believe there is enough dirt to cover and fill every hole a pair of healthy lungs creates / in the same way, that could be said about loneliness / that there aren't enough hands for everyone to keep / but even just the idea of the drawers between our fingers overflowing / is enough to decorate one's self with holes / and just as the sound of igniting gunpowder can drown out an entire religion / the shriek of air splitting to make way for me will take back the name / I have ever given to any god / and I will become an offering / in hopes you will whisper my name / like a prayer

gun—

an unnamed animal chained in a small yard.

A LOT ABOUT UNDOING

how many things have broken
in your hands as you hold them
ask the blushing night
how many stars have burst in

its palm. I have been thinking a lot
about undoing. I lose a tooth
and gain a phantom pain. I lose a
brother and gain a memory

I truly should have less
I have pulled so many
petals the soil asked me
not to touch

loss always gives back
loss always keeps our hands full

PARAMOUNT

a star seized & splintering

in a dark sea profoundly large

something like the love of a parent

or all the world's light—borrowed

both inescapable & unapproachable

how do you ask for something not

vital to your survival, but paramount

in unknotting its brilliances

mother, are you the sky—

could you just hold me

LITTLE CLOUD

that first person who saw the / Andromeda Galaxy / referred to it as
/ 'little cloud' / *little cloud* / breathing somewhere in infinity / orbiting
around its own beating / so far off one could not spot the rivers /
painting gullies in the palm of the night sky / grief / is observed in this
same way / given a name that defines it as small / as something with the
potential of being / both beautiful and fit to sustain life / fantastical &
gleaming / an entire atlas of constellations / a gravitational pull driving
to center / a spectacle, a race / buried too deep in wonder to ever
become an idea / the opulent comfort of visiting from a safe distance /
must one feel to know / simply by seeing I am / we do not remember
the name of the person who first saw this / little cloud / only that, in the
cool air of twilight / they could not turn their gaze upward / stare past
the atmosphere / and feel nothing any longer

IN THE MORNING I SO GENTLY SET
EVERYTHING I AM CARRYING DOWN

& place my palms
on the dirt in front of me

this is a sacrifice
this, a posture of giving

in all things I am reckless
but with my body I do not hesitate

it is all I have been given
seems a worthy thing to risk

& all I carry is just
a debt—this love,

those sweet wisps of hair curling
behind your ears like yawning clouds

someday I will pay for them
with my body or yours

and I am haunted by
not having a choice in the

matter. I've thrown myself
against whatever grief

pulls to the shore of my neck
and have received many bruises

in the shape of Xs
that I follow in search of

weathered treasure—*memories.*
anything I can keep in my

hands is empty weight
so take whatever bone or blood

is necessary to prolong
this living because I've certainly
given more for a lot less
nothing hurts as bad as

leaning your bones into joy
because it is borrowed

and at some point
it will all have to be given back

EULOGY

to wonder is to continue forward while the body waits

I am a multitude; an empty parking lot dressed in stardust; the echo and

the source of sound; raindrops hitting a windowsill and fragmenting—

I am each mirror, the body and its reflection; the name and

how it sounds when spoken to an empty room. I am always hopeful,

but rarely do I wield the damn thing. I just want to get home

before the streetlights turn off—I just want to get home before it gets dark

A GENERATION SWEATING BACK INTO THEIR SKIN

heart so full of oil my teeth are black / hands so full of myself I can't
bother with anyone starving / I cursed a multitude of endless summer
nights as a kid / now they only taste sour / I grasped at the tired corners
of their eyes / attempting to pull eternity out of them / I was told the
whole world could be mine if I bled for it / & that it was only desire that
created countries out of men / not purpose / I wanted to be warm—I
wanted to be sweet / so I drank until my lips dripped with honey / I
spoke the name of every person I missed so quickly they caught on fire
/ yet, I still withered / that darkness—its hands—they know nothing
of gentleness / drape streetlight around my shoulders / I got a long
list of friends that need its light / I spent the winter writing letters to
set beneath a bird's wing / and woke up one morning to sunbeams /
and promised myself that if anyone ever asks me for warmth / I won't
hesitate to hold them / I've watched an infinity of summer suns bleed
into a horizon I was so sure I would step foot on / and never did—I
can still taste copper / I was told for so many years that I mattered that
I actually started to believe it / I feel so soft in the morning / where is
there to go from here

tomorrow so far away I need a different tongue to speak its language
/ tomorrow so far away I need a map / night so full of bodies ain't
no place to sleep / dawn so hungry ain't no food left / arms so full of
myself / I have no place for you

language—

an unwrinkling of plagues.

~~TONIGHT~~ NOTHING'S ~~WORSE THAN~~ THIS PAIN ~~IN MY HEART~~

~~after "El Paso" by Marty Robbins~~

~~I~~ move pretty ~~quickly when I am giving distance / between myself and the man with the~~ gun ~~/ he who is giving more value to the ground he stands upon than I do / that man being anything that doesn't have a definable face / a people,~~ a tremble, a machine ~~/ I can keep everything I know to be holy in my mouth / names, fingers, stray strands of chocolate hair / my life exists in their thin and frail shadow / and I open my eyes each morning / only to kneel~~ in wake of their breath ~~/ if you~~ sculpt a ~~monument from sand / that too / I will revere and call to be moist and tame beneath my~~ tongue ~~/ if you call me to be, I will flow outward / and become a river—a terribly raging thing / almost always a pair of starving hands cannot finish what they wished to begin / almost always something is left half-alive and writhing / almost always / I once~~ co we ~~red within danger's shadow as it stood, rapping at my door / but now I have become that which knocks / I called distance to be a sea /~~ and drank an entire ocean ~~/ I have become that faceless thing guarding~~ hallo we d ~~ground / I imagine a bullet is fired each time I take a breath / and it is hard to believe there is enough dirt to cover and fill every hole a pair of healthy lungs creates / in the same way, that could be said about loneliness / that there~~ aren't enough hands for everyone to keep ~~/ but even just the idea of~~ the ~~drawers between our fingers overflowing / is enough to decorate one's self with holes / just as the sound of igniting~~ gun ~~powder can drown out an entire religion / the shriek of air splitting / to make way for me will take back the name / I have ever given to any god / and I never knew dying would call me to move the quickest / in its direction~~

CLEARSUNNED

daily, I am
haunted by
the absurdity
of my smallness—

how do I ever become more

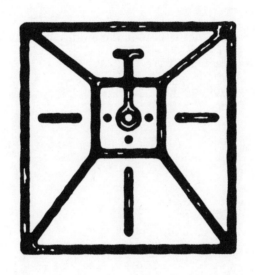

MOTHER'S DAY / NORTHWESTERN IOWA

in its waywardness

      flickering against a hollowing twilight

I consider the rogue patch of lightning

      perched

off in the distance

      momentarily nestled inside the mouth of a low hill

      just above a field of rye

to it, home is a revolving door

from drought to dance / to pride to affair / and again to drought

as an idea

home

is comfortable &

      comfort is indispensable

a guttural bellowing: the crank of distance collapsing to closeness draws

nearer

      its voice pressing to my neck

      the peach hairs

      saluting

it begins unfamiliar / before stumbling off

        like an echo removed from the racket that birthed it

the palm of mother's belly

        the organic rumble

the swell eclipses the longing

and the blanket of night

smothers everything golden

and new

HOPE, BREAKAGE, AND KNOWING

a wish is the bone, fractured

asking to be mended

hope is the bone

never learning

it can be broken

TO NOT QUESTION

it is in this way
the world is painted in whimsy

everything succulent seemingly
planted precisely just for me

I stare through atmospheres of darkness often
never have I seen a shimmer flicker out

eating a plum in pale twilight
skin dripping from summer's sultry whisper

distant light painting dark coins
on the lawn using only leaves

an entire kaleidoscope of disbelief
I taste everything my hands can touch

& wonder wildly beneath a moon
tethered in its own sea of darkness

it leaks over this entire kingdom
asking only that I admire what it brings

I am awash in temperate light and never question
whose blood paid for these freedoms

freedom—

choosing where to bury

beneath what grass

facing which cardinal direction

toward which home

recognizing the body

having the body

having the body to bury.

IN COPING WITH AN EMPTY CHAIR

I am as strong
as the heaviest things
I have failed to carry

a child, a whimper, a mouthful of wonder

I have abandoned all softness
all the groaning and groaning
I have left no room for
pain in my throat
I said a name one time, earnestly
and then never again
it dried up, as my hands
it tears the stockings my wife wears
it pulls moisture from the concrete
leaving empty streaks in my driveway

sometimes I wake up breathless
as though something has burrowed, following
the trail of my windpipe
a moist graveyard in between my cheeks, an acknowledgment
and I scream
and scream

until

it's four in the morning
and I am rearranging the darkness—strained
I am lifting and moving
just to feel strong again

just to wrap my tongue
around a name and
urge it to sound like something
more than haunting

like something
that can be held
in my hands

COUNT IT ALL AS LUCK

count it all as luck that today disease is more a word than it is a feeling

count it all as luck that things can be buried before they are named: that mourning begins at first light

count it all as luck that they found the vein on the third try and the gold is flowing

count it all as luck that time, as precious as it is, only bares its teeth when no one else is watching

count it all as luck to be born in an age in which there are so many distractions one has to remind themselves that they are wilting

count it all as luck sunbeams painted my plot in warmth and they will be the first hands to hold me without asking if it hurts

count it all as luck that yesterday was an ache still humming in today's chest

count it all as luck the sun whispered my name today as quick and soft as igniting gunpowder

count it all as luck that a breath will follow this one & this one & this one & this one & this one & this one & this one & this one & this one & this one & this one &

WAR PAINT

it always calls out to me

        lips pursed and wet

                that wanting thing

weary, I abide

        & strangle the color from dusk

                so as to paint its chest with

selecting a vibrant &

        threatening hue

                mostly, I choose

to live in wake of

        any one of the realities

                fear presents to me

going as far as

        using my own hands

                to apply its

war paint

THRUSH

find the dead and paint them lavender / everything can be / quiet and pretty / with the right amount of / disbelief / they will call me stardust / as I am sprinkled above water / remove me from my malice and / in contrast / I am remarkable / but *not here* / the gathered heads will wilt / and in whatever silence is politely coaxed from the stirring afternoon / a thrush will flap / its good wings / and recite my name

SURFACE OF THE SUN

I have been to Arizona—

listened to people geniusly relate the state to the surface of the sun

the ways we reconcile our suffering

little to no laughter

—red everything

brutal stardust

so unlivable, yet its population blooms each year

in line for therapy

—hello grief

I forgot to grab a number

when I did—129,784

yes, my mother used pills

no, in the living room

clear blue & stale air

not a cloud in the sky of her eyes

—10, I remember the bus ride home from school that day

it was late August

my new sneakers covered in a thin layer of brown film

beams of thick dust and Midwest light poured through the windowpane

the place was so unlivable

surface of the sun

IT IS LATE JANUARY AND WE ARE DRIVING SOUTH

after "Atlantic City" by Bruce Springsteen

a few miles outside Minneapolis   on a highway dressed in the white
chalk of salt residue   & my wife sits, face turned to the window
watching the landscape become an oil painting   & the sun lingers
longer these days   turning the sky a blue hue of green   before
sauntering off   & large things seem to pass in this way: in
one's own good time and without notice   & it is in the same way
these things are mourned   & Atlantic City is crumbling out of the
radio   & I, too, wonder if everything that dies someday comes back
& what are we capable of losing when we gamble on that hope   &
what is a hope if it isn't worth losing everything for   & I consider
the beginning   —that which began stretching out before me—
no one simply waited to die   they held on to living like it meant
something   & now we are all fantasy   obsessed with keeping
what we have never owned—time   we think we have time   we
think there will always be more   but time does not belong to us
time belongs to grief   see how it lends you a   morning & by
nightfall it falls back into its clammy hands   all we are given is the
fossil pulled up after seasons of erosion   & grief is a lot like snowfall
in the way it deafens   in the ways it can be expected   mortality
isn't a curse, it's a promise   and it covers everything in its sweet ash
& when a name becomes past-tense only the wind can carry it   & we
spend an entire life grasping onto that wind   & when my wife turns
her attention back to me and we talk there is nothing missing   & I
wonder if it is only in these small moments when we are alive—alive in
the way in which we are not grieving something   but celebrating—
which is so close to mortality their lips are touching

THE NIGHT MARTY ROBBINS HEARD THE MASTER'S CALL

after "The Master's Call" by Marty Robbins

he crumbled to the dirt and shouted / *oh God, these words I vow!* / &
haven't we all been there / at the intersection of death and deliverance
/ making the assurance that we are capable of change / no matter our
history / where does our allegiance lie / *fear, control, strength* / all are
wolves in sheep's clothing / an enigmatic fear / being terrified of the
dark, never having walked into it / never having seen its face / which is,
of course, your own / it is not the possibility of losing something / but
of the confirmation that it was us that had become lost / not a picture
of safety / remove guilt from my hands and I become spectacular / no
longer bargaining for more / yes, I am splintered like dry bark / desire
is a fruit / it has always been the sweetest thing / could there ever be
anything else / the section of the sky where light has to travel through
layers and layers of atmosphere is a mirror / what do you see there
that's worth dying for / skin dripping like a strawberry on the vine / or
tomorrow / its face buried in a dense cloud

desire—

mistaking a breath for wind.

A THIN PLACE

I am governed by lineage
my hands are doors ghosts pass through

I feel it all—
even that which I
haven't ever known

to say the thing that haunts
so many times it becomes a phantom pain
is an exercise in misunderstanding

mother's lilac tongue
bouquet of frolicking laughter
growing wildly on the shore of night
everything the light touches
is finite but holy
like a pressing of hands

when it touched your skin
did you shimmer
were you momentarily brilliant
as an exploding star
to remember you as such
is a song

you—as an exploding star
skin song
brilliant shimmer

momentarily touched
to remember you
to remember you
touched

everything holy frolics on the shore of night
growing wildly finite
mother's bouquet
pressing hands to lilac
tongue touches light

say the thing
the haunting
an exercise
a misunderstanding

all which I haven't known
is all I ever
feel

my ghosts are hands estranged from the body
I am the lineage governing this grief

AT THE HOSPITAL, A BIRD SOARS OVERHEAD

the pond outside the window glistens like a handful of coins
a pair of swans begin their second lap
from its wooded edge, drifting to the
opposite end—dripping with afternoon
light. they don't flinch when the stones
tossed by two young boys hit
the water and sink. a bird flies overhead—
so high that its shadow
blankets the entire hospital. your eyes,
sapphire blue, cloud and grow dull.
clumps of people walk by—
passing the open door. their heads
down; rushed, or facing
one another in noiseless conversation.
no one seems to notice how long of a night
rests beneath a bird's wings. I
glance over at your still skin—
your breathing buried deep
inside of your spirit. outside the
window, the swans finish
their lap, stones keep hammering
the still surface before finding
the pond's bottom—the swans
pay no mind to the clatter.
the world collapses only in
this way: when it is sure you are
the only one watching

bird—

a body suspended from its mechanics. a quiet rapture, like something
blameless plummeting out of the mouth of a harmless sky.

CONTROL

I don't believe there is much in this life we can control
we cannot force the clouds to part and make way for abundant light
we cannot will ourselves to someplace other than where we currently are
we cannot make people love us and worse
we cannot make people stay

we cannot make people stay

even if the space in our palm washes so perfectly around their tender
fingers
and our tongue wraps so gently around their name
it blooms into an eternity
we cannot make people stay

I lost my grandmother when I was young before I knew grief
before I understood what it was like to heave and become empty
she was the only person that would chase me around her two-story
home simply because she wanted to see joy in movement

we cannot make people stay

this is not about loss or grieving it is about empty spaces
it is about how quick we are to set a glowing screen in front of our faces
when an overcast sky haunts us
have you ever dipped your fingers in paint and pressed them to a canvas
because you wanted so badly to be a part of something vibrant
have you ever swallowed a sunset because you couldn't remember what it
was like for something beautiful to end and not have to mourn it
sometimes the empty space is a name that has folded into past tense.

sometimes it is beginning to understand how something so perfectly present can grow stale. sometimes it's about praying to a shadow.

this is about penance

shouting the name of what's become absent into the void it's gone to so you can wrap it in anger and guilt it into returning. have you ever dusted the headstones becoming weathered in your throat. do you even need to read the date engraved in old stone in order to wrap your hands around a pain that has made itself a home in you.

this is about reckless anger.

this is about space. do you visit yours? do you acknowledge it? do you honestly believe there could ever be something light couldn't soften? it is good to reconcile ourselves to our empty spaces. it's good to be at home in them. it is good to bring people into them. it is good to fill them with patient hands that filter the rocks from the soil and find water beneath.

this is about control. or rather, how little of it we have. I think what I remember the most from the little time I had with my grandmother is that we were never stationary. We never allowed anything to grow a layer of dust. When a space once filled with a body or a voice empties out, it isn't meant to become a monument of what once was. It isn't meant to grow dark.

this is not about empty spaces. there is so little we can control in this life. aside from how we choose to fill all the spaces that were once occupied and now lie empty. that now lie waiting to be tilled with bare hands.

this is about newness. and our ability to control whether or not we believe that it exists.

IN THE DARK, IN A ROOM OF STILL BODIES

grief is a communion

we take separately

but eat and drink together

NIGHT MOISTURE

give me a home / what I mean by that is / fill the silence with the warm
mist of your flailing breath / I know intimacy as a bird / delicate and
hungry / like a gun / kept beneath a pillow / who will hold me / I
am not particularly soft / I am more bone than anything else / more
flight than forgive / line my tongue with your name and I'll paint the
nursery / so the sun warms it like the palm of your belly / remain and
I'll build a nest with your bones / I'll lie there all winter / pressing the
egg into my cheek / pressing my mouth into the mouth you left for
me / checking for a pulse / checking for a body / how is it I can be
so rigid / so unmalleable / and create something breathing / that will
emit hot air dripping onto a lower back / filtering through the soil of a
garden behind an ear / I know intimacy as a stone / lying / unmoving
/ between root and moisture / a disturbance more than a welcoming
/ a slow and steady violence my bones are struggling to absorb / night
watches me tremble / a swollen moon sick with pleasure / and I am so
terribly tired

the body—

the hands are a field—carrying only lightning and its brief shadows. the
mouth, a crowd of memories—colliding and running into one another
in search of the exit. there is no exit, only unearthly flashes in many
different directions until you become ash.

ODE TO STREETLIGHTS ENDING IN GOOD COMPANY

to all of you who were beside me when my childhood screamed past
like birds migrating south through a cold evening sky as the first surprise
Midwest winter storm empties out its deep pockets over the city / *thank
you* / I carry your names with me like thin glass / intricate, invaluable,
fragile crafted artwork / at the time, I didn't know how to say *you saved
me* or / *this love is like a canyon in that it gets carved out slowly, tediously, and
it cannot be filled by anything short of holy water* / we, beneath streetlights,
claimed our city as a kingdom and called out our commands in bursts of
belly laughter / we, beneath streetlights, fought for our joy with sticks as
swords and the weight of sleep as our curfew / we, beneath streetlights,
shared a meal / well—you ate at your family table while I patiently
waited beneath a humming sun / a dull, orange haze / a breathless
light pushing back against the night / for you to bring me out a warm
plate of leftovers / you always offered me a seat at the table and I always
knew I would be welcome / you said my home is your home / but it
cannot be / my home is a bleeding dusk / my home is fit with a view of
taillights turning into driveways / my home is the smoke of my breath
wrapping around me like a blanket / my home is waiting / my home is
carving your names into tree bark / my home is watching from the street
as your father speaks so loudly with his hands that the windowpane
ripples with belly laughter / my home is borrowed joy / and when I
speak of my home to my children, to my wife, your names will be the
echo / that calls the walls to bow to their knees

joy—

a pinpoint of light across a violent gorge.

MY FATHER'S SON

I have become so callous / so rigid / my houseplants forgive better
than I do / while withering, they lend me a breath when a trying day
pickpockets my lungs / I see myself in the first yawn of morning / I see
myself there in the moon's halo / I watch it swell as night's knuckles turn
white / I watch and direct more air into my chest / I am confident / I
provide / my wife's hands are meant to hold nothing else / other than
what I have given her / full but lonely / my wife's hands / my covenant
to protect is a disguise for my desire to keep / see you will all be safe
here / hungry / but safe / is there anything left that still remains soft /
my wife's hands / I am as essential as the air in your lungs / I am trying
so hard to be warm / every wound I come across I form a bandage from
my own skin to set over it / but I am impatient / I am squeamish / I will
direct my hand to where the blood is seeping but you have to apply the
pressure / shield your suffering from me because I have seen enough /
compromise / my wife's hands / I am pragmatic / I am a problem to
anything in need of growth / because to me, that is linear / to me, you
cut off the hand to save the body / to me, everyone needs something but
I can't help them if I don't help myself first / how can I feed if I have
not been spoon-fed / my wife's hands / I crave order / I desire purpose
/ give me a river to drag and pull the pollution from / anything to kneel
into something murkier than my own breath / the whites of your eyes
/ a nickel in my pocket / worth is a funny thing / in how we delegate it
to only the things we want / forgetting what we have bled for / pulling,
strand by strand, the memory of longing from our crooked brains / oh,
to be gentle enough to only look outward / to not see the window / the
spotless pane of glass / but the trees behind it / the wind becoming so
small it runs its hands through their hair without pulling a single leaf /
oh, to recall every sweet thing that has dripped from your lips and not
forget how it tasted the first time it turned your tongue in a sanctuary /
my wife's hands

AFTER THE FIRST ROUND OF ELECTROCONVULSIVE THERAPY

it is my birthday / and mother is tired / she knows not what she says /
I ask her how old she is / she just repeats / in fervent prayer / that she
has yet to be born / what is air / why does it *haunt me* / always hiding
within itself / *I don't want you* / *I want what comes after you* / *the expanse*

I am to be exhumed from this body / azaleas in my fingerbeds /
something about undoing / something about never being ripe enough
to decay / I see your face in flowers / what of processes begin us / *I'm
sorry—my memory isn't what it once was*

I am so removed / my empty bone quiver / my flailing thunder tongue
/ catch me over your upturned hands / I am rainfall—you cannot have
all of me at once / but I am here for all of you / in her eyes I haven't
aged / as small as droplet of rain pulled into fragments on a windowsill
/ in fact, I have yet to be born

machine—

any toil dressed in purpose. immediacy mistaken for nourishment. its
only operation: to empty or be emptied; a bludgeoning.

DEPRESSION MEDICINE

I remember taking the pills—

chalky eyes of disparaging angels.

seedless fruits. fruitless orchards. grayscale lilacs.

momentum pulling every gulp of nothing to center.

writing a list of names like an impassioned ballad.

I remember your hands. your hair. your ferocity like winter.

whatever one can do to feel. *remember*

paint again the shadows buried beneath the tree dad was buried beneath.

paint again his smile poking up through fresh dirt like thyme.

I am promised tomorrow if I promise commitment.

six months for a brutal lifetime.

God laughs at this logic.

on earth time is a treasure; in heaven it's a weed.

I am promised I'll laugh again.

I don't understand this logic.

telling you about the world would be like holding the same note until

morning; like pulling stones from a river to build a new river; like exit

signs on the interstate with no ramps leading off.

moving forward like a breeze—maybe I'll smell like springtime if I keep

moving. maybe there will be someplace to pull off. to trust in this is

illogical, but how could the idea of having to survive yourself ever be

reasonable.

LAVENDER LINING

eternity
is a great pressing of hands
against light as it

> quietly washes itself in its own waterfall on soft marble &
> crawls down through tree canopy and swaddles weary spruce
> & sees its reflection and runs back to what bred it

see   it has skin

there are many things
I do not believe in
yet, they still happen—
the flower closing at night
and pressing its palms to the
sunrise in gentle prayer
asking to be filled with fire
this vulnerability happens only in quiet
like a shimmer; like a mirage
can thirst live here

all this dusk
with a lavender lining
as if to say—leaving, too, is
a gift
as if to say—to touch
is in itself
to bury

eternity—

a thinning place—where every longing is stilled.
a moonrise painted by every hand that has ever tenderly held you.

PIETY

we are all out
to sea
some looking for a
lighthouse
others, a current

THE FISHER KING'S HOLY GRAIL IS FILLED WITH HIS LONELINESS

heaven is a small room constructed

only of mirrors that we are lead to by a

vibrant body of light. per instruction

we are to stare into every

version of ourselves and ask every question

we lost sleep over and accept that silence is the

only answer

JUST ME, THE GROCERY STORE MUSIC

for Blake

& the neon

I am like you I say

flickering without resolve

see how I breathe

like everyone is captivated by it

how each tile dangling

from the ceiling by its fingertips

is a country

how the place that lives on the tongue

is both here and not

when I speak of where I first loved

it is a eulogy given to a living body, entirely

unaware it has one foot out the door

what is home but an idea

what is an idea but a light far off in the distance

a whisper, a serenity, a solace

in this way, I have had many homes

and in the starving mouth of night

I carve their coordinates into a smooth stone

& skip it over a vacant sea

FOR OTHER REASONS

who is stronger
the   mountain
—idle & firm
or me, born of
erosion—held
by hands that
only know how
to   take
how easy it is to
stand   still—&
be unchanged by
the   sky—it
has never once
given me a place
or a purpose—&
still, I have taken
its rain in my
open mouth and
said thank you
for not leaving
me the same way
you found me

LIKE MACHINES

what is this brilliance / a body so close / our breathing begins a flame / is this intimacy / the world starting here in our mouths / the only currency being whatever dust is left / from the rubbing together of our bones / the end of this could only be stillness / the hum of a past noise so loud it collapsed in on itself / is every wound on your skin a country / were the wars lost there deafening / no, we cannot be fixed like machines / there is no tourniquet for grief / only knowing / run your fingers over my neck like rainfall / sing your sorrows into my fault lines / swim with me in adoration beneath a moon drowning in its dark sea / tomorrow will still have an ache / and its arrival will render us wary / the only way out / is holding the silence in our throats / until it opens a door

moonbeam—

the glowing hair of my lover painted over my chest beneath a dark sea.

LEARNING TO THROW

what a good thing to be
young and to call the creek
behind your home 'brother'
and to be fed by the same

mouth and to spend the most
fragile summer nights wondering
how one becomes mighty
and when, if ever, we learn

how to swim in the bigness
we will eventually become
and if we will be able to remember
how to make it back home

and in the yawning light
of morning we will feast
on bright, breathing yolk
and feel a little bit closer

to calling ourselves strong

time—

row of feathers   the altar

is crumbling

I am lead here—   here is a

memory

have you seen it?   no—I can paint you there

recite

your name as though it is true   close your teeth

around its fingers   if you aren't a little scared,

no one

will hold you once you've gone   these soft things

never expire   leave the body behind   it knows nothing of

beauty   aside from what it fashions from bone   blueprints

from ash-soot ladders from ivory   none of that rubble   could ever be a

temple   the path veers

off here   like smoke broken by   wind

do not look

down

you'll miss   it.

PROJECTILES

what of silence isn't fragile—
      bursting in its own skin

in the fingernail sliver before
      my wife yawns herself awake

holding final words like a grenade
      slowly pulling the pin forever

I just want to sit for a moment
      let me remember without

all of this shrapnel

WHISPER

& its gleam is a fervent piercing

through the murmurs of night

I see it

& home has to be somewhere

in the rising and falling

of its slow breathing

GHOST MACHINE

no one purchased my freedom, it was lent to me spit out
like a cheap snack from a vending machine & every day I am
persuaded to return a little bit I just want to wet my lips
I just want to taste another sunrise
& feel it fizz in   my
mouth like   fireworks
If I knew it   wasn't
mine to keep I
never would've
taken it—
guilt is the
bullet made
by the ma-
chine &
I've
become
the gun

SO SMALL I CAN HARDLY BELIEVE IT EXISTS

at the great passing
what will be left
aside from the smoke
from the bones I
pressed my bones into

the friction of heavy laughter
the huffs of an evening
slowly turning the lights out
all of this and how endings unfurl
subtly and then all at once

I will remember your name
because I've spelled it out
on many occasions with flower petals
on the lawn. the honey is
still thick on my fingertips

I will crawl to my wilting
and leave a spectacular lesion
in the dirt
all tongue and no teeth
sauntering off into any accepting oblivion

a wispy shelf of clouds loosening its grasp on the horizon
this love is so brief
I can hardly give it a name in light of eternity
—but a freckle high on a cheek

a meteorite careening
downward to the ridge of the top lip
I will remember this
bury me
in the crater it leaves

SOMETIMES THE SHEEP DON'T COME BACK

I am trying to write a poem that doesn't say I'm sorry // but every curve is a fading half-moon, each line a trembling knee // my grace is a river with a deer carcass half-submerged at the source

the quickness of my guilt // it comes up on me like an animal that is larger than I am // understanding it has nothing to be scared of anymore

I am trying to write a poem that is a quiet act of revolution // like a river taking back a city; like every wall is only built to be ruptured

I—a drop: I—a sea to something small // I—an animal first feeling its prowess // I—an armory with an open door // my tongue a hollow-point

nothing ends as much as it unfolds into another becoming // so by the end of this I'll be a new flame on an old torch // lighting up a familiar darkness

MOONWRAPPED

after "Moonwrapped" by Richard Edwards

I will pile it all on top of each other / until it causes wound in the mouth
of an afternoon give me back all the names / I once couldn't rinse
from my mouth / place a sliver of late summer in my palm / watch me
poke its belly / until it spills all over / to feel anything at all / is a magic
trick / I am a kaleidoscope of missing / every face I once held in my
fingers is a shape / all of this is geometry / teaching me to memorize
/ the circumference of grief / set the crumbs of a stale morning on
my tongue / watch it swell / I am perpetually between two planes /
moonwrapped—leaking lavender & dreaming / waiting for morning
/ look at my stress marks—my mouth wrinkles / the nests pulling
themselves apart at the corners of my eyes / trace my map unto the
stars / see I am feeling

FROM MEMORY

God, recount for me the ways in which you are a bridge

the space between me and my memories

       seems so small

as though I could reach a finger

       and feel my old skin

              sun-stained and dressed in summer

       I am a fountain, no

I am water—fluid

       careening through my own makeup

like a creek in an underwater canyon

       DNA wrapped around its own tongue

              hungry for its own air

       this isn't the way back to euphoria

can I decide what I want to be remembered for

       it is dark here in this canyon

show the glittering of my tongue

       I, too, spoke a cosmos into place

              perhaps it's still spiraling

       all of this is to ask

if I have harbored hatred in my heart

       and it is true it alone can kill

will they all be waiting for me

      can the instances of good outweigh the rest

            can a future be built on forgetting

     I cannot show my hands

there must be another way in

     let me keep some of it—the *feeling*

this face—spilling

     brush off the rust

        a soft jewel in the shade

SOME WOULD ARGUE THAT THE SIMPLE ACT

of your heart beating without you ever having to ask it to is a miracle
while others would say it is simple anatomy and maybe sometimes living
is somewhere in that gray area between the two which means surviving
is a slope and sometimes you don't need to ask the beating thing to keep
rhythm but to convince the mouth to say thank you once in a damn
while / yes / maybe if my mother had found the voice needed for
worship she would have made more room in her hands for gratitude and
less for those bitter berries she plucked throughout the day and saved for
when her hunger grew stronger than her will / yes / some argue that
once you die your brain remains conscious long enough to know that it
has passed on and I wonder if gratitude could ever live in that space /
yes / I would take the side that having to ask the body to do something
as basic as turning the open palm downward is anatomy but doing so
when the thing being held is honey on parched lips is / yes / a miracle
and I would like to think that in that brief period between the haze and
heaven you would remember that I am still holding you

worship—

unfolding the name kept between your fingers, reciting it in a single note
to an ivory moon—waiting until morning for the answer.

NOT ABOUT A GUN

in a moment of vulnerability / I bite my cheek and taste metal / I give
my body to the cool breast of night / and what miraculous things it
does to the starlight buried in my dark / the sky weeps while no one
watches / morning is painted with streaks of red stretched lazily towards
the edge of the horizon / it is tired / and like us it has avoided pouring
out into some poor soul's lap / I see this and wonder / who could ever
want to pierce me / to create a hole / a sleeve to put an arm through
/ and I am reminded how some have such a vast reservoir of hate / it
could contain the whole unfragmented sky / God—I am exhausted /
from reading memorials / from keeping my head above the surface of
some unfamiliar sea of grief / what a strange pain to feel your lungs
expand / close to bursting / with the air of someone's last breath / if
we lit candles for every person who heard a pop in place of a goodbye /
and tasted gunpowder on their teeth in place of their lover's lips the sun
would blush / oh how red it would become at the sight of how small it
truly is / in light of the light that has been taken / in light of the light
it couldn't lend to replace and fill each darkened space / I am moved—
profoundly / by how much some people's arms can hold / by how
many crumbling bodies they can keep together at once / and, as the sky,
remain strong / until it is safe to press into the chest of twilight / and
empty themselves

WHAT IS THERE LEFT FOR ME TO LOVE

I have held each season in my hands / & they each have grafted their beliefs into my tender skin & I have all but found myself entirely unchanged / how does one become cherished / to the point they begin examining the overflow of their own heart / yes, your breathing is a bird drinking from a puddle / & I want to purify its waters for eternity / but I feel this the most strongly in autumn when each beautiful thing / becomes incredibly temporary / I say so much more than I know / how can this be honest? / when the days become so short I taste the moon on my tongue / I speak only of what has been / all of these ephemeral moments / seem to be strung together one after another and set to swing loosely / over the curvature of the horizon / what is there to grab onto when it all is so brief / your gentle breathing / the steaming porcelain mug at your lips / the unfurling flower pollinating the garden behind your ear / how can my fingers clasp onto this wind

MISGIVINGS

a winter bellowing

me, condensing into

something malignant but brutal

like a suddenly seized sky

frozen and no longer making

deposits or withdrawals

Tuesday morning

and the sun remains buried in the canopy

I pissed the bed

and the cat leapt off

to trap a mouse

bury it in the dark that is everywhere

there is a good corner coming up I can feel it

tomorrow will be the

same kind of beautiful trouble

like being perched in the refuge of an overpass during a downpour

—I am alone in this sliver of dark

but it's worse out there

THE SMOKE SLOWLY RISES AND BECOMES A CLOUD

I only want to survive long enough

to make it home before

the porch light turns off.

a suddening into darkness

what I mean by this, is

how long can I

wrestle my demons

before they get

the upper hand

part of me doesn't want to know

PRAYER

to whoever finds and unwraps

the prayers I wrinkle out

between breaths of smoke—

of all my smallest needs,

for my misery to be unfolded like

a wish lingers like a wasp sting

MID-AFTERNOON, IN THE BREAKROOM, STARING INTO THE PALE FACE OF MY PHONE

our wanting to be known is
        so vast, a cosmos could fit inside

I'm never certain of what I'm
        feeling, everything is a mirror

undeniably, this creek is an
        ocean to something small enough incapable

of seeing the other side. hope,
        to me, is a sea—drifting in a current

is my complete self looking for
        the reason—why must I begin in fragments

shattered glass cannot unsplinter
        itself. an ocean cannot unwrinkle its

currents. I write this because I
        am trying. the other side, a mirage,

where I stand and speak without
        trembling

SO MANY THINGS

are god or can be god. my
father turning away. my
mother turning over. my
relentless pursuit of more. my
endings and infinities—the
crease between them like a
tight range of mountains across
a thin bedsheet—even the brief
shadow cast by its looseness.
my wife & her fingers—when
they press against light it
shudders as though she made
it & loved it into being soft.
a stout mountain peak piercing
low clouds—the way is always
shrouded in a fog of unknowables.
god are you erosion—are you
anything so brief it is only
a memory being dismantled, brick
by brick, until its face
is soot

PORCHLIGHT

what if I never find the light
am I to fumble all the way through
the darkness

what if I never make it home
what if I never see the small
light crest a dark horizon
calling me home

TODAY, THE SUNRISE LOOKS LIKE IT CAN HOLD ME

one day I decided

to take a step

and it hurt less

than standing still

LINEAGE

I am a	whole moon	discolored and	sick with
lineage	a treasure	can never be	something
that isn't	lost	*a belief*	daughter, are you
breathing	without a name	I am not sure you are	*here*

A STRAY SUNBEAM FINDS YOUR CHEEK IN OUR THIRD-STORY APARTMENT

the trees are so small from up here. like

paintings on a large wall across the room.

my hand catches yours like a fire-wilted leaf

falling on cold ground. today, I am

feeling. to exist in a space where the

only watchful eyes are painted still—

seeing beauty is undressing time &

drinking its trembling breath—is to

want. the eyelashes of autumn flutter

against the chin of an October morning.

birds don't even know travel in this way—

piercing from stillness into brilliance.

screaming across a dull sky. the

rushing of our departure taking

them elsewhere. god's still eye

watches us build a country in

our mouths. He asks an ocean to

split and it opens—we could never notice.

possess—

when you are holding something beautiful

is it spectacular   or is it yours

it cannot be both.

MASTER OF NOTHING

I have climbed every mountain
keeping a dirt road from spilling
over onto the prairie and
I keep a handful of soil in

my pocket just in case I ever
stumble upon an unruly creek
that needs a king

the afternoon washes my
feet with its warm hands
and I become the mightiest
thing that has ever been this quiet

come nightfall, I will remember
the day's face and kiss its cheek
before the stars claim it as their own

I am the master of nothing
and I have never been so proud
to be so small

TO BE SPECTACULAR IS TO HAVE BEEN

after "Cancer" by My Chemical Romance

the incessant march of time leaves its shadow over everything

recall me only when I was most vibrant

July-afternoon blue like whimsy

post-twilight-thick-as-honey purple

lime-green eagerness

eggshell-white pith of agony

streaks-of-mauve-sunset painted on your lips the day of our wedding

violent-yellow bee sting that interrupted the message

glowing-crimson sheen of an apple plucked from an autumn tree

I am a collage of longing

a carnival of human fragility

sunburn-brutal-burst of the first summer peach dripping down lips

dripping-wet-silver of high hot clouds piercing the atmosphere

the imagined self is merely an outline

& how it becomes well-lit

is by getting drunk on

the wine pulled from the pulp

of the smallest loves that

split open and spill &

when our bodies fade into shading

they condense into a polarized beam

of excellent color to which we

recite as morning

IN THE DIRECTION OF THE MOUNTAIN I SCREAM

in an alternate universe
shame isn't the window
through which I see only myself

*

we build statues to fallen birds
and pray at their talons
brushing our eyelashes against their feathers
we just want to worship what
has kissed the sun

*

for what it's worth, I've
never seen the clouds
drop any god they've held—so
when we go to that
"someplace better" at
least it'll be safe

*

to birth—to believe something soft
can hold up the world
I am tasked to create a life from this rubble
my breath could never be god

*

all we know of death is its music
a single note held until it turns to mist
long, thin chimes in a gust
laughter bouncing off chest walls
an echo

*

mother, I've cast your bones
in silver and laid them at the
stone feet of my god—yet you
are still gone. what else must be
given   I have so little left
take this memory of you. *lilacs*
buried in brush—singing a welcome
to spring

*

nothing can be fresh without first
beginning the process of decay
see: the soul
how it begins as a sturdy beam of light
before turning to smoke
I am as steady as my tremble
when trying to say
the names of everyone I miss

*

what is beneath suffering
Joy: reverb. buried—always
beneath a grandiose racket
but in pressing my ear to the
underbelly of the laughter
I, also, harmonize

*

is there no space as divine
as the womb
surely the mouth must be close
it defines this magic
as living

*

this is all to say
there is nothing I am
trying to get over—
just some small
calamities I am learning
to carry

BENEDICTION

it is morning & I'm fine with this

despite the frequency to which

I state the antithesis

another day rarely brings something

devastating in totality

if that were true

I wouldn't be saying this

PITH

this mercy is bitter;
plighted   pith
sometimes I want
to be chained to
that thing calling
me to be smaller
s o m e t i m e s
freedom leaves too
much   for me to
want

WHAT MARTY ROBBINS MEANT WHEN HE SAID A WOMAN'S LOVE IS WASTED

after "Running Gun" by Marty Robbins

when she loves a running gun / is that there is a whole world here / and soft doesn't mean weak / you can put the whole sky in your mouth / it doesn't burn / not everything has to be a war / your body is not an instrument / set it down for a moment / look how the chest rises and falls next to windblown grass / see how there can be order / structure / and in that / utility / your body and its bridge / the soil / make a whole song when put together / yes, in a father's absence is left a void with a sailor's tongue / quiet it with listening / not matching the pitch of its screams / manhood is a country claimed by a servant hand / not a viper with a gun / some men fight wars for revolution / others find release in their fury / stay with me here / just lie down a bit / just stay and trust you are more than something left behind / you are something more than a casualty

LILAC

where does it all come from—the miracles

the strangle of need loosening its grip

the graying of color

frustration shredding beauty into bark

frustration like pressing a gun to a lilac's mouth

the bullet—an unsatisfying response

the brilliance of tenderness

could it ever become monotonous as water

could it be everywhere

could it—

IN THE DREAMS I HAVE ABOUT TORNADOES

the funnels pluck gingerly
as if picking carrots from their garden
I watch from a rooftop, safe
my hair whipping around as though
it's taking its first full breath
in the dreams I have about tornadoes
I am the moon—in the way it coaxes
twilight into sleeping to the sound
of its breathing standing patiently
behind the wheel of its dark ship
allowing the night to do what it
has always done: swallow whoever
stumbles into its open mouth
I think of growing up in a vacuum
all turbulence and violence
in the dreams I have about tornadoes
I am gritting my teeth, trembling
control is rainfall in a desert
the base widens and the horizon vanishes
the world flinches, I grin
and wake up with
dirt in my teeth

CROSSING THE BRIDGE RIGHT AT EVENTIDE

I fear my memory is fading like a tired oil lamp / crushed beneath the weight of a long night / every feeling is a phantom pain / I cup my hands to ease the ache and find only air / this is not a prayer / though my hands are raw and becoming pith / all I long for is a tree in the distance / I am neither getting closer to nor moving further from / though I watch the wind run its hands through the canopy / if I unfold into a choir of voices / and stand around every name I last heard recited like a song to an unmoved audience / will you all wake from a miserable dream / will I wake with you / your faces are beyond a wall of smoke / I reach out to paint the contours of your cheek with my warmth / your skin curls around my fingers like a wish / & dammit I am alone / but not in the way of being alone that I've outgrown / but in the way that I am learning we are never not alone / at our best, we are in a crowded room of ghosts swaying to unheard music / I lean into their twilight / they dip backward / I cry out / & it becomes an echo before the words leave my teeth / I am *alone* in the way that I will never be closer to you all than this shared agony

THE ROBIN FLAPS ITS GOOD WING

I go to recite your name
and a robin tumbles out of my throat

> with its good wing, it drags itself
> to a pond and drinks

so this is intimacy

I know every broken piece of you
the sharpened bone pricks my tongue

> a patience like a gun
> a stumbling through the breathlessness

an entire continent growing fruit that won't ripen

an eternity of watering not the half-dead
but the not-yet-fully-alive

> drown me in the ocean you hold in your mouth
> pluck the marigold growing in the soil behind your ear

the robin flaps its good wing and sings

sunbeams tumble out
from the underbelly of clouds

> twilight wrings water from my hair
> it sleeps to the sound of my breathing

SHIFTING GOLD TO VIRTUE

see the belly of night
distend after taking in another
body—the immediate response
dipping down to set
shimmering capsules on
shouting tongues
give me permanence and I'll return
it gilded—more tangible
I plant flowers in my garden
and refuse to open my eyes
until they bloom I place the petals in my palm
and grind them into the skin
how badly I long to become some-
thing vibrant. to grow into
something that can glow against
the darkness encasing it
I am trying so hard to hold
the stars in my teeth without
crushing them. to not see
every shimmering thing as
gold

NOVEMBER

gold is as much the weight / as it is the value / so carry only what you can keep in your pocket / this life / a great theft / time gives me so little / and I continue taking more while its head is turned / I just want to watch the leaves fall a little bit longer / & see them flame as they wither / I don't need much / that is all love is / a little patience here / a little attention there / accompanied by slow breathing / and listening to the air keeping it from plummeting / there is no grand exit I am asking for / just small moments of brilliant change / forever and ever / and ever and / ever / just enough to carry with me / when I go

BONE

oh, to be content
        give me breath
without the impurities
        of living /

the ache of
        not having
the burden of collecting
        the injustice of it all /

these sweet things
        become stale
before I find the courage
        to share them /

succulent afternoon
        dusk swelling to spill
morning so tender it falls
        right off the bone /

what I have felt
        has simply
not been
        enough /

watching a patch
        of low-lying hills
inhale a bloated
        late-evening sun /

nights—thick and
        rich with oxygen
a palette of shimmering
        drinking honey /

the offense concerning
        fullness: it becomes either
dreadfully uncomfortable
        or grows painfully temporary /

I am trying
        to hold on to things
that are more real
        than they are exuberant /

it has not been enough
        to convince me
there is anything
        that is permanent

CONCERNING THE EXISTENCE OF GUARDIAN ANGELS

I consider the night my two closest friends
sat at the end of my bed
turning a crystal nugget into smoke
I had just turned 14, they older; my *heroes*
I waited in anticipation;
I grew into the wall—silent
one passed out and the
other nearing, lifted his head
and with one open eye said *don't end up like us*

*

it was bitter cold. sister and I strapped
into an idling car in the garage
mother fiddling with the stuck door
lightning struck my skull
and thin smoke piled in
somehow we awoke in the hospital
comprised primarily of fumes
I have no memory of waking up
this tells me it was a miracle

*

I was 15, it was a warm April night
lying on a park bench beneath the hollow hum
of a lamppost, I counted my blessings

mother sipping green jello in a hospital bed
we were both uncertain about tomorrow
and in that way, we were together
birds began signaling a new day's arrival

*

I missed the first half of 2nd grade
our family relocated to a women's shelter
to me, it was a castle
the fence, a moat, the security door, a drawbridge
my mother checked us out so we could walk to
the diner down the block to have lunch
a woman ran in, her stone face wet and blue
she listened to the gatekeeper speak of options
as though they were miracles
I struggled to decide between the
chicken strips and chicken nuggets
in the end, I ordered neither

*

senior year, our entire small-town high school
attended the funeral of a girl who died
she graduated the previous year—she was beloved
classes were canceled for a few days
it was an apparent suicide and everyone
questioned what they could have done
to stop it, to help her
we circled around as her coffin was lowered
all adorned in black. all questions rose into

the air like smoke. only the sky was
dressed in white

*

a guardian angel is without a body
just a stream of wind carrying a name
keeping memory like hard dirt with
the imprint of something once alive
a promise sealed in smooth amber
on my best days, I listen to everything
on my worst day, I take silence as a guarantee
for more

~~CROSSING THE BRIDGE RIGHT AT~~ EVENTIDE

I fear ~~my memory~~ is ~~fading like a tired oil lamp / crushed~~ beneath
~~the weight of a long night /~~ every feeling is a phantom ~~pain / I cup
my hands to ease the ache and find only air / this is not a~~ **prayer /**
~~though~~ my hands are ~~raw and becoming pith / all I long for is a tree in~~
the distance ~~/ I am neither getting closer to or moving further from /~~
~~though~~ I ~~watch the wind~~ run ~~its hands~~ through ~~the canopy / if I~~ unfold
~~into a choir of voices / and stand around every name I last heard~~
~~recited like~~ a song ~~to an unmoved audience / will you all awake from~~
a miserable dream ~~/ will I awake with you / your faces are beyond~~ a
wall of smoke ~~/ I reach out to~~ paint ~~the contours of your cheek with~~ my
~~warmth / your~~ skin ~~curls around my fingers~~ like a wish ~~/~~ & dammit ~~I am~~
~~alone / but~~ not in the way ~~of being alone that I outgrew years ago / but~~
~~in the way that I am learning we are never not alone / at our best, we~~
~~are in a crowded room~~ of ghosts ~~swaying to unheard music / I lean into~~
their twilight ~~/ they dip backward /~~ I cry out ~~/~~ & ~~it becomes an echo~~
~~before~~ the words ~~leave my teeth / I am~~ *alone* ~~in the way that I~~ will never
be ~~closer to you all than this shared~~ agony

GOD SCULPTED FROM GRIEF

which of us is the clay / what I mean is who forms who / yes—after
a long day I make myself a cocktail and toast to whatever darkness
I am running from / but I leave the lemon slice in the ice tray / this
grief is erratic / arriving whenever it pleases / though to its credit, it is
revolving around a moving target / mother tells me stories from when
she was a teenager / handing out pamphlets at the Denver airport at
17 / before graduating to make LSD in the mountains / handing out
God like a prescription / a liturgy / before inventing her own / this is
forward progression / my tongue wraps around the same language / I
worship anything with space to hold me / at 17, I wasn't molding new
idols / I was calling any park bench a warm bed / —any garbage can
a vending machine / —any old friend drowning in chemical smoke a
prophet / I am trying to make crooked things beautiful again / dressing
them in words that don't describe what they are, but what they could be
/ mashing stardust into a cool, dark drinkable liquid / sharpening my
teeth with its misery / everything is malleable with these hands / I craft
this grieving / and polish it for sale

infinity—

a warm morning; clearsunned.
the door to home opening forever.

FATHER'S DAY / NORTHWESTERN IOWA

had I known my father, I could've loved him

some things are inseparable

tragedies cannot be strained from lineage

though they've held different things—we

share the same hands

my inability to nurture echoes his name

his drinking problem gave me a wide throat

you drink so fast my mother told me

that's the danger

I fill that tomb with appreciation

I've forgiven myself these many tiny calamities

and have learned to love myself—and in the same way

him

lineage —

the frail thread between understanding and forgiveness. a mirror
reflecting compassion onto innocence—a rapture.

WE ARE ALL GOING

into a night that knows
only departing
its mouth, a long
thin line of silence
carrying only our
unspoiled wishes
a summer, undying
and easy to carry; to be
strong and tall; to
never stumble upon a
reason to tell a lie
this reality is an organ
playing on the wind—
off somewhere
shimmering. a rich
and dripping sound
like pressing an
ear to fruit as it ripens
I focus on this song
like it is the largest coin
at the bottom of

a fountain. when we

become undone,

when we forget

about this galaxy

of softness,

everything becomes

urgent—a phantom pain,

feeling the echo of an ache

sometimes, I lament

after waking from

a pleasant dream

having seen it all

again. having been

so close to the

beginning of my

only tenderness

that I almost never

came back

LITTLE NOTHINGS

in my vault, I fill it with

heaven: *little nothings*

a long wind, frivolous

autumn painting portraits

on every empty sidewalk

the whole afternoon in fits

stumbling down busy

streets shouting over

traffic. bring me your color

if you're holding the sun

let me kiss its forehead

soft Everything

I want this to keep

long after it's set to expire

hold it tightly there

to your chest

lend it some breathing

some honey kept

from there in that small vault

HANDS FUMBLING

remember your grandmother's

brittle hands and how

delicately she held

the bouquet of wild-

flowers you picked for her

rest in the vibrant thread

that has kept you together

since you were young

hands fumbling to be

held and to hold

long before fear

claims the space

between fingers

WHAT IS THE OTHER NAME FOR BRILLIANCE

frolic
or is it movement
in all my inadequacies
hope is a thinning door
in the way I cannot pass through it
instantaneously
can anything ever truly change
I am all but a crater
I keep forgetting
I am breathing

light
I have forgotten
can anything be as pure
shrouded in darkness
without first losing
its gleam
and still keep its
whimsy
to wrap my tongue around it
pull me through the door

memory
bury me
as I was at my most troubled
everything is a mouth
so much of myself
is a beacon—
sturdy bones
that is the name
& recite it until
the key is laughter

HOW I LOVE THOSE ENCHANTING THINGS

like a moon swallowing a bay at twilight
the rocky outcrop of hills cupping this gleaming body in its palms

or the vibrant shade of green that melts through leaves when the sun bites
into them these things, beautiful, but their progression leads to loss

I could never forget their names, but the mechanics of pronouncing
them—the way I am supposed to cradle my tongue with my lips—this
will escape me

and I will be but a blubbering mess discussing some puddle becoming
hollow or those shadows delicately laid across the lawn like Persian rugs

no, this beauty requires a language rich enough to also cradle its
impermanence it needs rows of ivory to indicate in what direction to
eulogize its imprint

the clouds, how they blush before tucking their heads beneath the
blanket of night aswoon in the lust of longing—I, too, have been there

in that moment before it grows quiet

FAREWELL LANGUAGE

the face says it all

washed in light

the echo of laughter bouncing off the rib cage

the last few breaths huffing, thick with bravery

the flowers printed on the wallpaper pushing back against the wind

the machines keeping the blood flowing hum the most beloved
childhood song

God, if you are a noise, let it be this one

to have these notes removed from their original arrangement is a gift

—some only get silence

NO GENTLE FORCE

God—

      if you are a

      noise / let it be

spring rain   on the windowsill

      let it be an

      arrival

THE GRIEF I GIVE

when I am to pass on this grief—a quiet blossoming, a ravaging, an amorphous body—it will have a hue of laughter

ACKNOWLEDGEMENTS

To my friends, family, and readers, I am indebted to all of you. Your support and encouragement stay with me always. Thanks for coming to my events and readings, for sharing my work, for sending me poems, for asking questions, and for letting me put Marty Robbins on the queue.

Biggest thanks to Michelle Halket and Central Avenue Publishing for trusting and believing in my work. All of my appreciation for making this process joyful and memorable.

To Casey Knue, whose insight and friendship is directly responsible for this book coming together—thank you.

To Taylor Whipple, I'm always grateful when we are able to work on something together. Everything you do is a long, full breath.

To Chelsie, my wife—my now, my forever. Thank you for always guiding me in the direction of love and truth.

NOTES & CREDITS

"Moonwrapped" shares its title with a song from Richard Edwards's album *Lemon Cotton Candy Sunset*.

"To Be Spectacular Is to Have Been" includes an epigraph from the song "Cancer" from the album *The Black Parade* by My Chemical Romance.

"Tonight Nothing's Worse Than This Pain in My Heart," "The Night Marty Robbins Heard the Master's Call," and "What Marty Robbins Meant When He Said a Woman's Love Is Wasted" are written after songs from the album *Gunfighter Ballads and Trail Songs* by Marty Robbins.

Thanks to the editors of the following journals in which the following poems first appeared, sometimes in different versions.

8 Poems: "In Coping with an Empty Chair"

Back Patio Press: "Tonight Nothing's Worse Than This Pain in My Heart" and "Little Cloud"

Detritus: "Piety"

Empty Mirror: "Birthday"

Ghost City Press: "Surface of the Sun"

Honey & Lime (Oceans & Time): "Night Moisture"

Kissing Dynamite: "October, and Everything Is Breathing"

Lyrical Iowa Anthology: "Master of Nothing"

Okay Donkey: "In All My Memories Flowers Are Taking the Place of Faces"

Oxidant Engine: "Mother's Day | Northwestern Iowa" and "Some Would Argue That the Simple Act"

Revival Magazine: "For Other Reasons"

Royal Rose (The Castle): "There's Got to Be More to a Human Being Than That" and "Outcomes"

Semicolon: "Not about a Gun" and "Shifting Gold to Virtue"

The Shore: "How I Love Those Enchanting Things"

Turnpike Magazine: "Thrush"

Unvael Journal: "Control"

William Bortz (he/him) is a husband, poet, and editor from
Des Moines, IA. His poems appear in *Okay Donkey, Oxidant Engine,*
Empty Mirror, honey & lime, Turnpike Magazine,
Back Patio Press, The Lyrical Iowa Anthology, and others.
He is the author of *Shards* and the chapbook
The Sky Grew Back with Clouds.

Growing up, William spent time in foster care, in homelessness,
and in shelters. His aim in writing is to explore how joy lives in
uncertainty and mourning.

williambortz.com
@william.bortz

Bestselling poetry from Central Avenue Publishing:

coffee days whiskey nights by Cyrus Parker

Confessions of Her by Cindy Cherie

2am Thoughts by Makenzie Campbell

Sincerely, by F. S. Yousaf

shades of lovers by Catarine Hancock